UNDYING DEDICATION

The Story of G. P. Bowser

R. VERNON BOYD

Gospel Advocate Co.
P.O. Box 150
Nashville, TN 37202

UNDYING DEDICATION
Copyrighted © 1985 by Gospel Advocate Co.

All rights reserved. No part of this publication may be reproduced, stored in a retrieval system, or transmitted in any form or by any means without the prior permission of the publisher.

Published by Gospel Advocate Co.
P.O. Box 150, Nashville, TN 37202

ISBN 0-89225-281-2

Gospel Advocate Biography Library

The Story of G.P. Bowser
Undying Dedication

R. Vernon Boyd

Gospel Advocate Company
P.O. Box 150
Nashville, Tennessee 37202

The Story of G.P. Bowser
Gospel Advocate Biography Library, 2001

© 1965, Gospel Advocate Company

Published by Gospel Advocate Co.
P.O. Box 150, Nashville, TN 37202
www.gospeladvocate.com

ISBN: 0-89225-281-2

Undying Dedication

CONTENTS

Acknowledgments
Introduction
Chapter 1—Background and History 15
   Birth and Early Years
   Methodist Beginnings
   Early Days in the Christian Church
   Beginning in the church of Christ
Chapter 2—Educational Efforts 31
   The First Christian School
   The Silver Point Community
   Silver Point School Begins
Chapter 3—Extracurricular Activities 43
   Bowser Home Life
   Summer Travels
   Worship in Those Days
Chapter 4—Further Educational Efforts 57
   The School at its Zenith
   Silver Point School in Decline
   Southern Practical Institute
Chapter 5—Bowser's Quest Continues 69
   The Move to Louisville
   Bowser Family Matters
   Two Disciples

Chapter 6—A New Endeavor 81
Fort Smith and Levi Kennedy
More Travels

Chapter 7—The Fruits of Labor 91
Bowser Christian Institute
Detroit
Fort Worth

Conclusion

ACKNOWLEDGMENTS

My life has been greatly enriched by being exposed to the work of a great servant of the Lord. I am grateful to Thelma Holt and her family for the cooperation I received as I sought to educate myself in an area of church history unknown to me and my background. G. P. Bowser truly loved the Lord and his church and sought to give it leaders who could effectively serve after he was gone. His vision looked beyond the harsh realities of his own time to a better day for the Lord's people. I am happy to donate the proceeds which I might receive from the sale of this book to the cause of Southwestern Christian College and its work for the Lord in fulfillment of Bowser's dream.

Beside my indebtedness to Thelma Holt, from whom most of the information for this book came, I want to thank Michael Case who researched the work of the Silver Point Institute, many former pupils and associates of Bowser who shared freely their admiration of the man, and especially Anita Owen Harkey and David Conley whose artistic ability helped me to tell the story of significant events in Bowser's life where no photographs remain.

INTRODUCTION

There have been two outstanding leaders in the twentieth century among black members of the churches of Christ: Marshall Keeble and G. P. Bowser. Keeble was much better known among white Christians, but Bowser pioneered in leadership much earlier and left a tremendous legacy of ministry and Christian education. Both men began adulthood around the turn of the century. They worked together in the beginning stages of the Jackson Street Church of Christ in Nashville, Tennessee when it broke away from the traditional Christian church.

As their careers in the church of Christ developed, Keeble came to be identified more with the white church interests. On the other hand, Bowser was unhappy with the racial prejudice in whites, and so committed himself to work within the black church. Thus he lived in poverty, for most blacks at that time were poor. Bowser's greatness was a result of his keen mind, superior education, and his zeal for the Lord.

Keeble came to prominence several years after Bowser's pioneering work in Christian journalism and Christian education. Keeble was a master at

INTRODUCTION

communicating the simple truths of the Bible. Following the example of Jesus, he could illustrate his message through the use of everyday parables. It is estimated that he baptized as many as forty thousand people into Christ, and many considered him to be a better preacher than Bowser. But Bowser was more scholarly and had great sections of the Bible memorized. Reuel Lemmons said that Bowser "was a clear, logical, cool thinker."[1]

In 1902, Bowser started the *Christian Echo*—the only national publication among blacks in the churches of Christ. It still serves numerous churches today. He is also remembered for his work in beginning the first Christian school for blacks in the Jackson Street church building in 1907. He worked tirelessly for the rest of his life in various educational efforts which aimed at training the ministry. His life's work resulted in the formation of Southwestern Christian College in Terrell, Texas, and earned him the title of "The Father of Christian Education" among blacks in the churches of Christ.

---

[1]Reuel Lemmons to Vernon Boyd, 30 March 1978.

A TRIBUTE TO WHOM TRIBUTE IS DUE

Jesus said and I quote, "And whosoever of you will be the chiefest, shall be servant of all." (Mark 10:44). As minister of the Strathmoor Church of Christ in Detroit, Michigan, and now of the Oakland Church of Christ in Southfield, Michigan, brother Vernon Boyd continues to be a servant to many.

When brother Boyd asked me to talk with him about my parents, the late George Phillip and Rebecca Bowser, I was delighted to share my thoughts with him about the life and times of my parents, whom I considered my closest and best friends.

I deeply appreciated brother Boyd's interest in their struggles and their desire to train and educate young people as my father put it, "from the cradle to the grave, in the way of the Lord, more perfectly."

Brother Boyd was also interested in their struggle in the work of the Lord's church and it is a joy for me to remember the many changes for the better that I have observed in the congregations and in the

Christian schools and colleges within our brotherhood.

And now I am most grateful to be able to express my sincere thanks and admiration for brother Boyd's book, *Undying Dedication*. The academic excellence and accuracy of the research is a tremendous credit to G. P. Bowser, the Bible preacher and scholar. And more importantly, brother Boyd's work furthers the cause and enhances the importance of Christian education.

In Christian Love,

Thelma M. Holt
3516 10th Avenue
Los Angeles, California 90018

Undying Dedication

CHAPTER 1

History and Background

Birth and Early Years

George Phillip Bowser (usually called by his initials, "G. P.") was born February 17, 1874 in Maury County, Tennessee, about sixty miles south of Nashville. His maternal grandfather was Frank Sowell—a pioneer preacher of the Christian church who had preached extensively in middle Tennessee until his death by drowning when his small fishing boat capsized. Bowser's mother, Charity (she changed it to Cherry) Elizabeth, married Thomas Bowser and was a member of the Christian church. Thomas and Cherry Elizabeth had five children. G. P. Bowser was the youngest. Because of many factors, hard times continually gripped their lives.

When Bowser was too young to remember, his father and a friend were smoking tobacco in a pipe when a spark accidentally ignited a can of gun powder. The blast killed Thomas. With the burden of five children to raise, Bowser's mother was determined to have her children succeed, so she provided them with a good education. Although she was considered to be uneducated, she knew how to read and write—talents which were quite unusual for a black woman of that time.

UNDYING DEDICATION

After the death of her husband, she moved to Nashville where the Methodist church had an educational system for blacks known as Walden University, a Freedman Aid school founded by northern whites for Negro students.[1] It offered a better education than the public system at the time and gave schooling from elementary grades through college. She did various domestic work to support her family. So intense was her desire to provide for her children that she even searched the city dump to find a pair of unmatched shoes for G. P. to wear to school, much to his embarrassment.

In Nashville she attended the Methodist church—partly because of convenience, and also because of her appreciation for the educational advantages it afforded her offspring. Consequently, she raised her children in that tradition. However, she retained her membership in the Christian church of her childhood.

Bowser later reflected about having been raised a Methodist. The doctrine he learned taught that a child's parents—in Bowser's case, his mother—bore the sins of the child until twelve years of age. At that age, the child was expected to begin an individual spiritual journey toward heaven. Bowser said he was glad he did not die before age twelve because he felt he had done enough sinning to send both him and his mother to hell!

In spite of his early indoctrination, Bowser seems to have been a spiritually sensitive person. When he reached the age of twelve, he went in regularly to the mourner's bench and there prayed for the

BACKGROUND AND HISTORY

G. P. Bowser

receiving of some sign from God regarding his salvation. He had been taught that such seeking would produce some powerful effect in his life, and then he would know he was one of the elect of God. For three years he sought the Lord through prayer and meditation. So persistent was he, that after a while he began to doubt the kindness of the Lord because he perceived no response to his earnest entreaties. Some of his friends seemed to receive that for which they sought with comparative ease. Not so with him.

Finally, a Baptist preacher helped him by saying that if a person was sorry for his sins, all that was really necessary was to state that fact before the church, and tell of his love for Jesus. Bowser did this and seemed to satisfy the church leaders. He simply arose from the mourner's bench and announced that he had religion. Perhaps he was less convinced than anyone else, because "conversion" was not as thrilling an experience as he had heard many others relate. He was assured that while some were powerfully converted, some were more moderately so, and others even less moderate. He concluded his was the latter variety. But his experience joined him to the Bethel African Methodist Episcopal Church in Nashville in 1889 at the age of fifteen.[2]

Methodist Beginnings

Within a year of his "experience", Bowser became a class leader in the Methodist church. In 1893, at age eighteen, he became licensed to exhort (make talks). He also developed an active interest in a particular young lady in the church whom he had known from Maury County. She had also

BACKGROUND AND HISTORY

moved to Nashville, and was known as Francis Rebecca "Fannie" Billips. She was five years older than Bowser and already had a child when his interest in her developed. Her father, too, had died when she was quite young and her mother—a half-Indian—was an invalid. Fannie's education only went through the fifth grade because of the need to help her mother by working. Her older brother promised to help her go to school if she would come and live with him and his wife in Nashville, but schooling never materialized for her. Fannie had a very good mind, however, and taught herself so extensively that many people assumed she was much better educated than she actually was.

She was very pleased to see Bowser developing in the Methodist church because she was a devout member and made a habit of reading her Bible and praying daily. Bowser had recognized that he was not considered handsome by most standards. However, he reasoned that he was not responsible for this and that the Lord would provide for his needs in due time. The fact was that he was very black, which was considered terrible and ugly. Yet he seemed to have an inner strength which was quite appealing—especially to Fannie.

She was quite popular as a student and had a beautiful voice which she displayed in the Methodist church choir. For a while, Bowser had some stiff competition in courting Fannie, because she was actively pursued by a porter who worked on the Nashville-Jacksonville train. In those days, a porter's position meant good pay and security within the black community. Bowser learned the schedule for the train so he would know when the porter, Mr. Blocker, would be in town. When Blocker was in Nashville, Bowser made himself scarce at Fannie's house. Whenever Blocker left for work, Bowser went back to Fannie's and enjoyed the tropical fruit which Mr. Blocker had brought her from Florida. Through frequent visits and love notes, Bowser was finally able to win Fannie's affection.

During the days of their courtship, Bowser had a tragic accident which affected him for the rest of his life. Fannie and Bowser were hurrying across a railroad yard one night. They waited for one train to pass, and then he dashed across the first track. A train on the next track coming from the opposite direction struck him. It pulled him down the track and broke his leg in two places, leaving him with a permanent limp. His left arm was so badly mangled that it had to be removed a few inches above the elbow.[3] Naturally, it was quite a shock to both of them, but it did not seem to dampen their love. Fannie still wanted to marry Bowser and she did so on June 25, 1896. Bowser was twenty-two and Fannie twenty-seven.[4]

Since Fannie was active in church, she was aware of his budding reputation as a leader in the Methodist church—much to her pleasure. Bowser once noted with a sense of humor, that in spite of her religious involvement, she was far from holy. And for many years afterward, he still would not vouch for her sanctity!

Since he was licensed to exhort—which was the first step toward becoming a minister—he studied

BACKGROUND AND HISTORY

When Bowser was a young man courting Fannie in Nashville, Tennessee, one night they were late going home and were rushing across the train track after a train went by only to dash in front of a second train on the second track going in the opposite direction. Bowser was lucky to escape with his life. The train caught his arm and tore it off. He had only a short stub of an arm for the rest of his life.

diligently at Walden University and was admired by his fellow students and teachers. He eventually mastered five languages in addition to English: Greek, Hebrew, French, German and Latin. Most of these were probably learned during his time at the university.[5] In 1895, when he was twenty-one years old and finishing school, he was honored to be given a charge from the presiding elder to preach in Cleveland, Tennessee. This meant he was to have his own congregation! He was thrilled.

But whatever enthusiasm he had for the job quickly vanished once he got there. The pay was extremely meager and not enough to support him and his family. After six weeks, he decided he was going to lose his wife if things didn't change. Notifying the presiding elder of his departure but not waiting for an answer, he and Fannie immediately set out for Nashville. With no money, they hitchhiked and located some transient work in the process. Thus they managed to get back home.

Although the experience in Cleveland was mostly unpleasant, entering the ministry had brought him to a more intense interest in the study of the Bible. There was so much about the Bible he wanted to know that he sought every means he knew to satisfy his thirst. He became interested in the teachings of other churches. A Congregational church minister gave him an Almanac Discipline containing a summation of their doctrines. It did not seem to please him. And for some reason, Bowser had gotten the impression that Baptists were selfish, and was not much interested in learning about them. At one point, he would have considered no religion at all, except that his overwhelming belief in God would not let him rest. So he searched further.

Before too long, despite his misgivings, he

BACKGROUND AND HISTORY

teamed up with a friendly Baptist minister named George Davis, and held a tent revival on Kayne Avenue. It was during this revival that an old minister by the name of Sam Davis dropped by each afternoon. They visited and discussed the Scriptures for quite a while before evening service. Sam Davis was well-acquainted with the Bible, and answered questions with plenty of quotes.

One day Bowser asked him if he knew of a church which taught the kinds of things he said, and he sent him to the Christian church. There were two such groups meeting at that time in the black community—one on Gay Street and the other on Lea Avenue. Bowser liked what he heard from the old man and was more pleased as he learned of the way the Bible was preached and practiced by the Christian church. He was sure that his old friend and minister at the Methodist church would appreciate his new-found knowledge. Since Bowser was respected at the Methodist church, he assumed he would be eagerly received to teach his new discoveries there. Reverend Turner, however, stated that he knew all about the "Campbellites" and would have no part of it.

As time went on, Bowser studied the Bible with others from the Christian church and brought questions to the Methodist bishop for answers. The result was that those to whom he brought questions announced that he was not a Methodist any longer, since he seemed to believe the things about which he spoke.

This presented an entirely new problem for Bowser. Up until this time, his religious inquiries had been considered a healthy quest for knowledge, but now he found that his quest to attain the Methodist bishopric was no longer possible or even desirable. The greatest hurdle to be faced, however, was that of his wife. She, of course, was a dedicated Methodist, and was unprepared for the news of his departure. He later said in describing their marital relationship that when she decided to give him a piece of her mind, she rarely stopped until she gave him all of it! No doubt this was one of those times. Bowser determined, however, to do what he felt was right before the Lord as best he understood the Scriptures.

He felt he had no choice but to be baptized into the Christian church on Gay Street in 1897. Fannie eventually came to accept the inevitable and later was baptized also. He was twenty-three years old and had been married less than a year when this transition occurred.[6]

Early Days in the Christian Church

As noted earlier, there were two groups related to the Christian church in the black community. Lea Avenue was the more exclusive congregation which openly catered to the light-skinned Negroes and shunned those of a darker hue. This group was known for its very popular minister, Preston Taylor, who was a successful undertaker and businessman and was often requested to speak at many civic functions. He was light-skinned, indicating his racially mixed heritage. Anyone with white "blood" was respected in the black community. The

BACKGROUND AND HISTORY

When he and Fannie were just married and he had graduated from the Methodist school in Nashville, the Methodist church sent him as preacher to Cleveland, Tennessee where they stayed for a few weeks. With few members and little support, he decided to return to Nashville and give up preaching. As the couple had no money, they hitch-hiked through the mountains of east Tennessee to come back to Nashville.

jingle circulated in this context: "If you are white, you're right; if you're black, get back; if you're brown, stick around." Sometimes white fathers provided generously for their racially mixed children although they would not be publicly identified with them. This church obviously preferred the elite because of its padded pews, carpeted floors, and beautiful music—both choral and instrumental.

All was not as well at Gay Street—a less wealthy congregation. But despite its seeming wealth, Lea Avenue, its sister congregation, was experiencing turmoil. This was a time when brethren were having heated discussions regarding the use of instruments in worship, clubs, and missionary societies in churches. A strong voice against these practices was raised by Sam W. Womack, Alexander Campbell—two black Nashville preachers—and others in this fellowship. These men felt a kindred spirit in David Lipscomb, the white editor of the *Gospel Advocate* and president of the Nashville Bible School across town. Lipscomb was not only against these practices, but he also scorned the dividing of Christians into separate groups along color lines.

It was from Womack and some of the other brethren that Bowser learned several points about the Bible which he used in comparing it with the Methodist Discipline. It was natural, then, when these men decided they could no longer be comfortable with the teachings of the brethren at Gay Street and Lea Avenue, that Bowser joined them in the formation of a separate worship in February, 1900. At first they met in Campbell's home on Harder Street. Then they were able to buy a small building once used by slaves as a kitchen for the old Keeble estate which was owned by a white family. This facility, purchased in 1906, had also been the old Fisk University Student Center and was located on Jackson Street in north Nashville. The church became known as the Jackson Street Church of Christ.[8]

Fannie complained that Bowser was going "from limb to limb" and this instability bothered her as much as his leaving the Methodist church. For a while he continued to get invitations to preach where brethren were using instrumental music, but they usually would not use the piano or organ out of respect for his wishes. He tried to encourage them away from these aids and toward being more like what he believed was the New Testament church.

Beginnings in the Church of Christ

During this time Bowser was earning a living by means of different occupations and trying to find his niche in life. They were living in Ohio when Bowser's twenty-month-old namesake died of unknown causes.[9] In Ohio, Bowser operated a drug store for a while. It may have been during this period that he learned how to be a printer—an occupation he practiced frequently for the rest of his life. At some point, he studied under a rabbi, learning how to type and mastering shorthand.

Bowser's education was more extensive than many of his contemporaries. It was certainly far beyond that of many of the older generation who had been born in slavery or shortly after slavery was abolished, when little or no schooling was available to them. Sometimes in churches, he would be the only one in the assembly able to read. Bowser was quite learned in religious studies, having read widely in denominational writings. But he was especially intense in his study of the Bible. He memorized large portions of it and delivered them so eloquently that it was commonly believed that he had the entire New Testament memorized.

Once in the fellowship of the church of Christ, Bowser found himself surrounded by devout disciples who knew and loved the Bible, but few with much of an education comparable to his own. His friend Sam Womack was a certified teacher and both of his daughters had graduated from Fisk University. After moving back to Nashville in 1902, Bowser lived on Justin Street directly across from Marshall and Minnie Keeble—another young couple in the congregation. Minnie was the daughter of Womack. Her husband never got beyond the seventh grade, but Minnie was able to help him educationally as he needed it.

The Bowsers and the Keebles saw one another regularly at church and were often together at other times during the week. Their children grew up together as the best of friends. Keeble operated a small grocery store and delivered coal to customers on a route in a wagon pulled by a mule. Occasionally, he was asked to preach. He was also the treasurer of the Jackson Street Church of Christ. Keeble owned his house—one of the nicer ones of the area. It had a front porch, a large living room and a nice floor plan indoors. In contrast, Bowser's house was rented, and was what was called a "shot-gun" house—straight as a gun barrel from front to back with one room right after another.

BACKGROUND AND HISTORY

The appreciation which Bowser had for his own education and the deepening love for the Bible which had led him to this point reinforced his desire to encourage the younger generation toward a quality Christian education. He soon became keenly aware of the lack of teaching materials available to his brethren. He noted, too, that there was little communication between congregations. This led him to establish two things for which he is most remembered today: a school and a journal.

Bowser began the journal, *The Christian Echo*, in 1902 when he was twenty-eight years old and had been in the church only about five years. Shortly after his conversion, he began to travel among the churches and preach. He recognized that the churches and individuals within it were scattered and that there was very little contact between brethren, except between local congregations.

So he bought a small hand press which he kept in the kitchen of his house on Justin Street. With his one good arm, he ground out the early editions of *The Echo* and mailed them to churches and individuals. Bowser missed not having literature in churches because he had become accustomed to having it in the Methodist church. So he was determined to work toward providing literature for the brotherhood as soon as possible.

[1]Annie C. Tuggle, *Another World Wonder* (n.d.,n.p.).
[2]Thelma, M. Holt, *Life and Times of G. P. Bowser,* (Nashville: Associated Publishing, 1964), pp. 1-2.
[3]Interview with Thelma Holt, Detroit, Michigan, 10 April 1972.
[4]Tennessee State Library and Archives, Davidson County, Microfilm reel 475, Book 11, p. 16.

UNDYING DEDICATION

[5]Interview with Virginia Elizabeth Brooks and Thelma Carter Haight, granddaughters of Bowser, Detroit, Michigan, 18 April 1983.

[6]G. P. Bowser, "As Ye Find Christ, Walk in Him," *Gospel Advocate*, 46(34 March, 1904):190.

[7]Alexander Campbell, "Work Among the Colored People," *Gospel Advocate*, 51(2 December 1909),1523.

[8]Forrest Neil Rhoads, "A Study of the Sources of Marshall Keeble's Effectiveness as a Preacher" (Doctoral dissertation, South Illinois), 1970,58.

CHAPTER 2

Educational Efforts

The First Christian School

On one occasion when Alexander Campbell, G. P. Bowser, and Sam Womack—the dynamic trio of leadership in the black church[1]—were in the presence of David Lipscomb,[2] the discussion turned to the need for a Christian school for blacks. Lipscomb was supportive of the idea, but knew he couldn't financially assist in such an effort. He already had the responsibilities of getting his own school established and stabilized. He suggested to these black leaders that they begin an effort first, and then he would do all he could to help.[3]

So in 1906, when Bowser was thirty-two years old, a meeting was held in Nashville to set up a school. Sam Womack, a certified teacher, was very enthusiastic in his encouragement to begin the school. Womack's daughter, Philista, a graduate of Fisk University, was also eager to help. Bowser took the lead in setting up the school in the Jackson Street Church of Christ. It opened on January 6, 1907. It was a modest beginning, with nine pupils including Bowser's own children. All the teaching was done by volunteers, since there was no money to pay them. Ministers in the city came in to teach the Bible and other subjects in which they were qualified.

By February of the next year, the enrollment had increased to seventeen.[4] The year beginning in January, 1909, saw the school's enrollment up to twenty-one pupils.[5] The men asked for donations from all possible sources to keep the school effort alive. P. H. Black, a prosperous black builder in Nashville, was very interested in the school, but the financial support he was able to give is not known. He and his wife Sue did not have children of their own, but were kind enough to take others' children into their home in order to help them go to school.

The Silver Point Community

With the modest beginning in the Nashville school, a dream was born. From then on, many would strive to offer Christian education to blacks comparable to that offered to whites by white denominations and the churches of Christ. Bowser and Womack continually searched for further ways to bring this idea to completeness.

After living in Nashville, G. P. Bowser first came to Silver Point with Sam Womack. It was the custom of the Laurel Hill Church of Christ in Putnam County, Tennessee, to invite a preacher in every summer for a meeting. Womack was invited almost every year. He was probably the most capable and best-known preacher among blacks in middle Tennessee at the time. He and Alexander

EDUCATIONAL EFFORTS

Campbell traveled widely among all of the black congregations.

The area of Silver Point was in a remote section of very hilly country near Cookville, about 75 miles east of Nashville. It was a place where two roads crossed as they wound their way through steep hills. The location was also a railroad stop for the Tennessee Central Railroad. The community consisted of a couple of stores, some churches, and two school buildings (one for whites and one for blacks). The white school building was much nicer than the one used by the blacks, but it seemed not to have been in use much of the time. Besides the Laurel Hill church building, there was a church building for the Methodists and one for the Baptists.

The residents of the community were unusual in that there seemed to be several white people with a mild attitude toward race. This was quite different from the attitudes of many other parts of the South. In Silver Point, some whites, but not all, openly admitted that a black relative was their cousin or aunt, etc., and visited and socialized freely back and forth. This was in sharp contrast to the nearby town of Baxter which had very bitter opinions against blacks. There it was rumored that a rape or murder had been committed by a black man and consequently the town was openly hostile to any blacks entering its territory.[6] One time after the school began, a student's package came from home and was delivered to a Baxter address with the same family name as the student. Bowser had to ask one of his white neighbors to go and pick it up for fear of upsetting some of the townspeople of Baxter. But in Silver Point, the white people were tolerant and peaceful.

The Laurel Hill building sat in the middle of a cemetery and was very old. It was serving a twofold purpose for the extensive black population scattered throughout the area—as a meeting house for the church and as a public school. Four months of public schooling was funded by the county if a teacher was available.

The elders of the congregation—Henry Clay, Joe Beasley, Bill Johnson, and John Anderson—kept the church going throughout the year with talks and lessons. The highlight of the year was the preaching during the meeting at some point during the summer. It was a great time of Christian fellowship with large crowds, dinner-on-the ground, and much socializing. When Sam Womack introduced G. P. Bowser to preach in 1909, Bowser's delivery was so electrifying and positive that the church was "amazed."[7] Some referred to him as a "war-horse." As a result, the elders asked Bowser if he would come and be their preacher. He was persuaded to do this when he saw all the little children who came from those hills in desperate need of more education than four months of school a year. He wanted them to have Bible training, too. Bowser had a special love for children and they seemed to like him, too.[8] He kept gum and candy in his pockets for them at all times.

Since he had already helped to start the school in Nashville, he was familiar with the methods of beginning a school. He went to the school authorities

EDUCATIONAL EFFORTS

A gathering of faculty and students of the Silver Point school in 1913. This photo was taken from *Another World Wonder* by Annie C. Tuggle.

in the county seat of Putnam County and secured the contract to teach the public school at Silver Point. Arrangements were than made to move the Nashville school there. The brethren decided that the old building in Silver Point was inadequate and conceived the idea of rebuilding and expanding the facility. So during the summer, the brethren tore

A photo of the only building remaining from the Silver Point Institute. This is now the church building for the Negroes in Silver Point, Tennessee, and it was built with the help of A. M. Burton and other Christian friends. The frame building which once housed the school was located a few yards left of this structure and a separate building for the print shop was located in between the two buildings.

down the old building and built a new one about a mile away upon the top of a ridge in Silver Point. It was a two-story, clapboard structure in the middle of an eight-acre parcel of ground. All this was done while Bowser went about preaching that summer and recruiting students for the new school. He also received some financial support for the school from white brethren.

The new building was designed to house Bowser's family and some of the male students in dormitory fashion upstairs with a chapel area and classrooms downstairs. Other students lived in nearby homes and walked to school. The new building was not insulated and cold winds could blow through cracks in the walls. Mud was temporarily used to seal cracks, but when it dried, it retracted and fell out. A pot-belly stove and long wooden benches comprised the school furnishings. There were oil lanterns on the walls for lights. These were necessary, for there were many evening activities such as programs, debates, and preaching.

The Silver Point School Begins

The Silver Point school was scheduled to begin its first term in the fall of 1909. Bowser was to be the teacher for the public school portion which normally ran from August to December. Then his industrial school was to run from January through April. There was a fee of $6 per month for room and board for those who could afford it.[9] The first name of the school was "Putnam County Normal,

Industrial and Orphan School."[10] Later it became the "Silver Point Christian College" or perhaps more commonly, the "Silver Point Christian Institute."[11] Henry Clay of Silver Point, and Sam Womack and Alexander Campbell of Nashville served as the board of directors.

When the building was completed and Bowser and his family actually moved in and began school, everyone was elated. They were all proud to be a part of this effort in Christian education. Even the black children and parents who weren't members of the church were happy at the prospect of a good school under "Brother Bowser" as they called him. He settled in as a respected educator and got along very well with people. Soon they discovered that he also was a valued advisor if there were any papers to be filled out or documents to be interpreted or signed. This was useful when World War I began because he assisted young men—both white and black—in filling out conscientious objector papers if they were opposed to killing in war.

The main building of the school was on a grassy hill in the center of the school property. It's only source of water came from a spring at the bottom of the hill, and the water had to be transported to the building in large buckets. The new building, like the old one it replaced, was heated by a wood or coal stove. The stove-pipe was vented through an open window pane, but this did not always work too well. If the wind blew from the wrong direction, there might be more smoke inside than outside. But even so, Bowser was content with his surroundings.

He once responded to a co-laborer when something didn't go right, "I don't like to complain to anyone concerning my condition. I have always liked to do all I can to help myself and then if I see that I can't make it, I believe I would be justified in asking someone else to help me."[12]

Bowser proved to be a good man and a good principal at Silver Point. He was able to gather a fine group of workers around him. At first, he was assisted by Miss Lillie Gipson as a teacher. Fannie served as matron, cook, and laundress.

Bowser never turned anyone away from school. People were never too old or too young for him to try to help them. He believed in Christian education from the cradle to the grave. As the older pupils became more advanced, he allowed them to help teach the younger ones under his supervision. He was very patient in his teaching and went over subjects slowly and carefully until they seemed easy for pupils to learn.

In 1913, the ninth grade was the highest grade taught at the school. Classes were offered in Bible, algebra, English, history and Latin. The school had frequent visitors, usually church leaders, who were often asked to bring a lesson in chapel.

Some of the students were allowed to work their way through school in the printing shop. The second building to be erected on campus was a one-room building which housed the printing press used in publishing the *Christian Echo*. It was a small structure, not nearly large enough for all the activity which went on in it. Winnie Garrett[13] was a young girl from a church family living about a city block away from the campus. She, like so many of the other pupils, earned her education by working in the office from 3:00-5:00 each afternoon. She learned to set type and operate the new press which Bowser bought for his building. It was a press operated by a foot petal.

Harrison Ramsey was put in charge of the printing operation as assistant director. Type was set by hand for the *Echo*, a new song book called *Choice Selections*, and tracts and booklets used in the school and in evangelism. When in good operation, Bowser simply turned the materials he had written over to Ramsey and the print shop did the rest of the production work.

[1] Earl Irvin West, *The Search for the Ancient Order*, Vol. 3, (Indianapolis: Religious Book Service, 1979), 180.

[2] J. E. Choate, *Roll Jordan Roll: A Biography of Marshall Keeble* (Nashville: Gospel Advocate Publishing, 1968), 23.

[3] S. W. Womack, "Among the Colored Folk," *Gospel Advocate* 60 (3 January 1918):18.

[4] G. P. Bowser, "Work Among the Colored People," *Gospel Advocate* 50(20 February 1908):125.

[5] S. W. Womack, "Work Among the Colored People," *Gospel Advocate* 51 (28 January 1909):121.

[6] Interview with Mrs. Ethan Dunn, a native of the area, Detroit, Michigan, Fall, 1974.

[7] Winnie Garrett, who became Mrs. T. H. Busby, left a record of the school's beginning with her daughter, Mrs. Walter Balloon. Writer interviewed Mrs. Balloon, Detroit, Michigan, 12 April 1983.

[8] Interview with Evelyn Christian, Detroit, Michigan, 13 April 1983.

[9] Jack Evans, "The History of Southwestern Christian College, Terrell, Texas" (Master's thesis, Texas Western College, El Paso, Texas), 1963, 5.

EDUCATIONAL EFFORTS

[10]G. P. Bowser, "Putnam County Normal, Industrial, and Orphan School, Silver Point, Tennessee," *Gospel Advocate* 57 (29 July 1915):744.
[11]Tuggle, *Another World Wonder,* p. 43.
[12]Tuggle, *Another World Wonder,* p. 47.
[13]Idem, Balloon.

CHAPTER 3

Extracurricular Activities

Bowser Home Life

When Bowser and Fannie arrived in Silver Point, the children accompanying them were Thelma, age seven, and Lucille, age two. Clara, their oldest daughter, had been sent to Fisk University, which she did not like, then to Lane College in Jackson, Tennessee. There she met and married William Scaggs on April 30, 1907, so she was not a big part of the work at Silver Point. Before the year was out, their daughter, Philista, was born.

It was not long after coming to Silver Point that Thelma wanted to be baptized. She was taken down to the stream where the ice had to be broken on the surface in order for her to be buried in Christ. Then, she went on to become a vital part of the work with her father.

Because of the nature of their role with the school, others became a part of the Bowser family. G. P. never turned anyone away who came—some with money and others penniless. Those who had no money were taken into his own family circle.

On one of his summer preaching trips to Arkansas, he came across a nine-year-old boy whose mother, like Hannah of the Bible, wanted the young man to be brought up in the service of the Lord under a man of God.[1] The boy's father had died shortly before Bowser's visit. She allowed Bowser to take the boy to raise. His name was Richard Nathaniel "Nate" Hogan and his grandparents were pillars of the church in Blackton, Arkansas.

Bowser taught this bright young man the Bible. When Nate was just about thirteen years of age, he began to preach. The people in the audience—especially those about his same age—snickered through his ten-minute talk. But he was better than most young preachers and before long, he gained the reputation of "The Boy Preacher" as he traveled with Bowser.

Since the Bowser "family" was always large, Fannie became an expert in stretching food to feed whoever was present. Things were lean much of the time, but none of the boarders were ever put out of the house. She learned to be flexible and accept the life she had decided to lead when she married "Bowser" as she called him. Gradually, she became good at begging food supplies from people. Since most people had a garden, raised chickens, and killed hogs and the like for their families, she became adept at asking for whatever she saw and needed. She was a likable woman, and her purpose was to assist Bowser and his school, so people could not refuse her.[2]

At mailing time for the *Echo* each month, everyone present was drafted into the action of printing, folding, addressing and mailing. Fannie, who never felt she had prepared dinner unless there was dessert, often had to forgo that part of the meal because of the amount of work involved with the *Echo*.

Fannie had a very hot temper which exposed itself often. When she was mad, she screamed at Bowser in a manner easily heard all over the house. Bowser never yelled back, but patiently waited for her to finish and then calmly continued to discuss what he felt he had to do. She reserved her greatest anger, however, for anyone who criticized her husband. She didn't spare fussing at him, but she never allowed others the same privilege. On one occasion she met a gentleman whom she considered to be running over Bowser. She told the man that Bowser would not speak out in his own defense, but she would whip the man if he did not retract what he had said about her husband! The man, who weighed close to three hundred pounds, was evidently impressed because he soon made peace.

Once, when a family member asked Fannie why she stayed so long with such an ugly little man, she replied with hands on her hips, "He's the best-looking man God ever made!" She had developed a deep affection for him. It was a hard life they shared together—mainly because of poverty. She must have realized that Bowser could have taught school or done a variety of things for a living if he had chosen to live a secular life. But she knew he felt a higher calling and she accepted it. It seems she never tried to persuade him to go into anything else. She was a dedicated, faithful helper.

G. P. Bowser standing before one of his preaching charts and his wife, Francis (Fannie) Rebecca, holding the Bible.

By disposition, Fannie was a neat housekeeper and kept things quite clean. Bowser seems to have been the opposite. She constantly had to struggle with him to keep him presentable. He often dressed like a tramp and wore "'gator shoes" with rubber in the sides. He liked white shirts which had detachable celluloid collars—usually discolored and dirty from use.[3] He also did as little as possible to his nappy hair. Since his travels took him away from home quite a bit, his clothes often were ragged, unkempt, and unclean.

Summer Travels

When school closed each spring, Bowser traveled and preached all over the country. He not only had a passion for lost souls, he also recruited new students and financial support for the school. It is practically impossible to locate a black church today which was in existence then that he did *not* visit. Some churches called him for "protracted" meetings. This meant that they went on as long as prospects seemed good and he was baptizing people, or until he had to leave for his next appointment.

Sometimes it happened that a white brother exposed a black person to the gospel. If the effort resulted in a convert or the prospect of converting, it usually meant that a search resulted for a black preacher to come in and hold a meeting in order to establish a church. This became a frequent pattern throughout the South and was the origin of many black churches in the vicinity of local white Christians who broke the color barrier.

Traveling seemed to be in Bowser's blood, and he did so on every opportunity. One day he happened to be in Marshall County, Tennessee, without a car, horse-and-buggy, or any other means of transportation except his two crippled legs. He inquired about the local black community and discovered that the members of the church were conducting a funeral down at the cemetery for Andy Purdy, a strong faithful disciple and the only member of his family in the church. The brethren did not have a building or any place suitable for holding the funeral service, so they had assembled under an oak tree in the cemetery.[4] He began walking toward the location and arrived just as service was about to begin. Frank Fishback, the preacher for the few disciples in that part of the country, was there to conduct the funeral. Bowser walked up and introduced himself to Fishback.

Although they had not met before, Fishback was familiar with the name and asked him to conduct the service. Bowser agreed. As Bowser began to speak, he quoted many Scriptures which he felt would be of comfort to the sorrowing group. His knowledge of the Bible and his ability to quote extensive passages without opening the Word impressed those assembled. After the service, the brethren huddled to discuss his preaching for them while he was in the area. The Presbyterians refused the use of their building because the Holt family had recently left their fellowship to be with the New Testament group. Brother Holt rode around the country to the three commissioners of education and obtained permission to use the school building for three nights' meeting. This Holt family was to become one of the most outstanding church families in this century due to the many preachers which it produced.

EXTRACURRICULAR ACTIVITIES

Attendance at the new church was good and included many of the Presbyterians, but they remained unmoved in their beliefs. The preaching was outstanding. Bowser's usual practice was to hold up his hand in front of his face as if he were reading from the Bible, and then quote passage after passage to establish his points. He greatly strengthened the church on that occasion even though there were no converts.

When Bowser traveled, he sometimes took part of his family with him. His daughter Thelma remembers when she was four years old, going to Oklahoma City to visit Bowser's sister. She was a school teacher there and had married a Methodist minister who became a presiding elder in Oklahoma. Even with one arm, Bowser drove the car, washed, bathed and dressed Thelma. He did everything except comb the little girl's hair. He got some woman in the congregation to do that.

Thelma remembers playing with Indian children in the neighborhood and being impressed at the prosperity of her aunt and uncle. Since Bowser's only son died in infancy, Thelma fell into being his young "chief assistant." She was allowed at three years of age to stand by her father's knee when he preached. Later she learned how to set type, operate the press and the other steps necessary in putting out the *Echo*.

One summer the entire family traveled to Jasper, Alabama, where Bowser wanted to start a congregation. There were no members there. Most of the large black population was Baptist. Bowser did not seem to have contact with any white members of the church whom he could ask for help.

UNDYING DEDICATION

Bowser had almost the entire New Testament memorized and would customarily hold his one hand in front of his face as if he were holding his Bible and would quote extensively from the Bible.

So he set up his tent and began to hold services. Before long, he began to make converts. This upset some people to the extent that they burned his tent to the ground. Fannie became quite nervous and wanted the family to leave for their safety. A few

EXTRACURRICULAR ACTIVITIES

blacks spread rumors even among whites. They said that Bowser had come to town with a new religion which intended to change things quite a bit. They claimed that Bowser was telling blacks to get out of the kitchens of the white people and not work for them anymore. Some of the white people came to investigate these charges. Bowser assured them that he was not saying anything of the kind, and noted that his wife worked in a certain white man's house doing his family's laundry. He quoted the passage "If any will not work, neither let him eat." He convinced these men that he was a Bible preacher who felt he must preach what the Bible said. His message did not include rebelling against whites.

That night at sermon time, Bowser nailed his blackboard to a tree and continued the meeting without further incident. Some of the white people who had seen the great pile of laundry which Fannie had done also came out to the meeting. Fannie was good at the difficult task of ironing out the starch in men's white shirts. They saw this. After the meeting, Bowser asked the now trusting white men to go speak a calming word to Fannie. They did better than that. They came back with some food and money to show their appreciation for his godly efforts. They all shook hands as friends, and Fannie was relieved. Bowser stayed long enough to make a few converts and helped them to get a place to worship. Then he moved on.

UNDYING DEDICATION

Worship in Those Days

Worship has always been a social event—especially in the era in which Bowser preached. It was a time people felt elevated and uniquely bound together. People looked forward to going to church and wearing their "Sunday best" clothes. It was such a big social occasion that it is doubtful that everyone came with spiritual motives in mind. There was much visiting, courting, and horse-trading to be done and this was the ideal time. This, of course, was before television. There were very few radios and most of the country was rural. There was no concern about a service being long, because people did not get together very often and they seemed to want to be with one another.

People lived long distances apart and had no telephones. They came in wagons, on foot, and a few had buggies. In those days, having a rubber-tired buggy was considered quite a luxury. Not much thought was given to the quality or length of the sermon. There was usually no printed literature, and people just studied from the Bible. Bible school consisted of dividing the assembly into three groups: adults, young people, and children.

There was always a lot of singing, even though there were no song books. If there was a break in the service, after a while a sister who felt like singing would break into song and others would join in. Bowser found as he visited around that the groups did not sing very well—especially without books. Although he was not an accomplishd singer, he managed to teach a few tunes. He was led to use his printing press to provide song books to the churches. He put together the words to some songs he knew and called it *Choice Selections*. Once he used this hymnal with the churches, he usually left them singing better than when he came. In any event, worship time was always a special time for most all who came.

Some Sundays would boast a dinner-on-the-ground with everyone bringing food. It often was hard to have night services because of the distance people had to travel. Many had to get home to milk cows or feed the stock. However, it was convenient for all to stay and eat together in the middle of the day. Everyone gathered about 9:30 or 10:00 in the morning for Sunday school. Usually the group would stay together until about 1:00 or 1:30 in the afternoons. With that length of time together, there would be plenty of time for singing, praying, talking, or whatever. After the preacher delivered his sermon, if any brother wanted to make a few comments about how much he enjoyed the message, or tell what he got out of the lesson, he was free to do so. Of course, there were always announcements to be made. Since people were together so little, they enjoyed the association, and never rushed through anything.

Should there be a baptism, it was necessary to go to a creek nearby. Usually everyone went. Even making the good confession in the church building was a time of rejoicing. People left their seats, gathered around the person putting on Christ, and offered expressions of warmth and congratulations. Similar encouragement followed at the creek bank as the person came up out of the water, and was received into the fellowship of the church. Again, there was no rushing. When the congregation extended the right hand of fellowship to a new convert amidst tears of joy, it was a happy day for all.

There was quite a bit of evangelistic activity going on among the white churches during the thirties and forties. It was usually done with a tent being moved from place to place. When these tents were not in use by the whites, the blacks were able to borrow them for their efforts. Blacks and whites were free to attend one another's meetings. The seating arrangement was always segregated, regardless of who held the meetings. Separation was sometimes done with a rope down the center aisle.

In those days, speaking was an art. If a person was good at it, he often was invited to display his talents. Bowser was invited to denominational churches to speak and, on the other hand, if a denominational preacher came to where Bowser was preaching, he gave him the courtesy of saying a few words. But Bowser did not hesitate to speak the truth about the New Testament church wherever he went. He did not belittle people, but would aggressively pursue truth as he saw it. He showed many a person the weakness of doctrinal positions by use of the Scriptures.

This was also the era of debates. Bowser often got members of denominations so worked up that they would get their preachers out to answer what was being taught by Bowser in the community. Because Bowser was usually better read and was constantly quoting the Bible in support of anything that he mentioned, he frequently had others in a rage rather quickly. Bowser believed the Bible was "sharper than any two-edged sword" and he used it to divide truth from error. Thus he engaged in many debates.

In those times, preaching was entertainment as well as instructive. Verbal pot-shots were par for the course. A formal debate might grow out of questions posed during a gospel meeting when visitors were given an opportunity to question the teaching at the end of the service. These were times when a hot-head questioner would interrupt a sermon with protests or even threats. It took a strong public confidence to meet these challenges, and Bowser was a master craftsman at his trade.

[1] Interview with R. N. Hogan, Chicago, Illinois, Spring 1968.
[2] Idem, Evelyn Christian.
[3] Interview with Mrs. D. J. Bynum, Detroit, Michigan, 29 October 1973; Interview with John R. Flowers, Detroit, Michigan, 26 April 1978.
[4] Interview with A. C. Holt, Detroit, Michigan, 25 September 1972.

CHAPTER 4

Further Educational Efforts

The School at Its Zenith

While summers offered a stimulating change of pace, the needs of the school were never far from Bowser's mind. The new location of the school in Silver Point focused new interest in educating the blacks in the church but it also meant increased expenses. Bowser reported in February, 1912: "It is sufficient to say that it is now the best in its history." But he quickly reminded the readers of the *Gospel Advocate* of the great need for financial support.[1] In July of the same year, Bowser made a trip to raise five hundred dollars for Silver Point Christian Institute.[2] By spring of the following year (1913) he reported "the most prosperous year of the school."[3] However, he went on to note:

On account of the number of appeals being made and the unwillingness of people to help, I have decided to not make further appeals in behalf of our work. We hope however, as our work progresses, it will grow in favor with those endorsing a Bible school among colored people.[4]

As word of the new school's existence spread throughout the brotherhood, those interested in

Bible study came there to learn—even adults, both male and female. Bowser encouraged girls to come in order to become Bible teachers and preachers' wives. Three older students who came to learn were T. H. Busby, Alonzo Jones, and Annie Tuggle.

Busby, a widower who lost his wife and children in a plague, became very useful because he was talented in music and could help with the singing. Jones had a wife and two small children, so they all lived upstairs in the dormitory near the Bowser family. As a result of a gospel meeting Bowser held at Capleville, Tennessee, (near Memphis) Annie Clay Tuggle, a young school teacher, decided to come to Silver Point in the fall of 1913. She later became a vital part of several successful efforts in Christian education among the blacks. She was a beautiful part-Indian and had long flowing black hair. She came to the institute to study the Bible. She took classes in the highest grade offered—the ninth—although she was already a certified teacher and had taught school two years. She developed a thorough knowledge of the Bible and was effective in speaking.

In her book, *Another World Wonder*,[5] Tuggle tells about an incident that occurred when she and some other pupils went with a preaching student to visit a Methodist church for Sunday worship. The young preacher, C. W. Baldwin, called on her to answer a question from the audience. Surprised by the call to speak in church, she nevertheless answered the question by quoting Scripture. When she returned to school, she asked Bowser if she had done the right thing. Much to her relief, he assured her that she was not usurping authority over a man in that case.

After school closed in the spring of 1914, Tuggle was commissioned as field agent for the school. Since money matters were so pressing, she volunteered to serve. She was a woman of confidence—some said arrogance—but well-suited for the task. Since she was an older student, she had her own car and was free to travel. By far the most significant stop she made for the school was the visit to David Lipscomb, President of the Nashville Bible School and editor of the *Gospel Advocate*. The visit occurred during the last few years of Lipscomb's life and he was very ill. But he was still the best-known and most influential person within the churches of Christ. Lipscomb's wife, Maggie, restricted visitors to his bedside. She was hesitant, but after hearing the worthy cause, Mrs. Lipscomb allowed Miss Tuggle to see him. Lipscomb was touched with the twenty-four year old woman's plea. Although he did not personally have any money to give, he said he had some friends who did. He promised to do what he could for the school.[6]

He contacted A. M. Burton, president of the Life and Casualty Insurance Company. Burton had an undying appreciation for Christian education which he had never had. After founding his insurance company which specialized in selling low-cost policies mainly to blacks in Nashville, he became increasingly succesful financially and he was generous in his giving. Burton arranged for S. P. Pittman, a teacher at the Nashville Bible School, and

J. S. Hammonds to investigate the school. It is presumed financial help came later.

The years from 1910–1914 were years of increase for the school. Womack reported seventeen students from other counties enrolled and a total enrollment of forty-four in the spring of 1913.[7] By the end of school term in 1914, Bowser reported that fifty-seven enrolled and that the two-story frame building was free of debt.[8] Although the building was paid for, the visit by Burton and Hammond on January 5, 1916, indicated things were in a bad state of repair. Besides the two-story school building, the black brethren had built a brick chapel building and had begun a home for Bowser which was being turned into a girl's dormitory because of the pressing need for housing of students. Both of the latter buildings, reported Burton, needed extensive work done, at a probable cost of $750 and $200-$300 would be needed to equip them.[9]

Response within the next few months was significant—enough to allow both Bowser and Womack to be encouraged that the school would be permanently established.[10] Churches and individuals alike gave to the school. In the summer of 1916, announcement was made of an expanded board which included four white brethren and five blacks.[11] And so the school reached it's zenith during the 1915–1916 school year.

Silver Point School in Decline

At holiday times, the school usually put on special programs. Bowser utilized more of his talents

FURTHER EDUCATIONAL EFFORTS

Beside the Silver Point Church building a wooden building was built to house the press used in printing the *Christian Echo*, a church publication begun in his home in 1902. Besides having a better press than before, Bowser believed in training the children in some skill and the trade he knew best to pass on to them was printing.

on these occasions and often wrote and directed the entire operation with various students doing the dialogue or recitation.

Another aspect of his ability is seen in the required examinations which licensed teachers had to pass periodically for state certification. Bowser had a keen mind and never had any difficulty taking the exams all on the same day instead of spacing them over a few weeks as was allowed. The school authorities seemed satisfied with his competence after a while and gave him a permanent certificate which no longer required such testing.

With the new monies coming to the school as a result of the appeals encouraged by Lipscomb and Burton, a $1500 brick school building was erected, replacing the wooden building first built. P. H. Black was the contractor for this construction and he was assisted by Robert E. Campbell, the son of Alexander Campbell.[12]

In 1916, two teachers came from Nashville to help with the school. They were Mrs. Alexine Page and Mrs. Adline Brown. They were needed because of the increased enrollment. But increased enrollment also meant increased expenses. As spring term ended in 1917, little was said about the school in the *Gospel Advocate*, the usual reporting vehicle to the white brotherhood.

In August of 1917, S. P. Pittman wrote an article urging support for the school. He stated that the school could be a great mission for reaching blacks, but prejudice and bigotry were hindering such.[13] Bowser wrote a month later because school was ready to begin and the institute continued to need support. He agreed with Pittman in assessing the real problem. He noted that the chapel building had been completed and another school building was being built.[14] It is hard to ignore Bowser's earlier remark about not wanting to make constant appeals for money, but rather allowing the school to commend itself because of the quality of performance. Bowser was becoming increasingly discouraged that the white brethren, who had money for their own schools, did not see the need and

FURTHER EDUCATIONAL EFFORTS

While the Silver Point school was operating with quite a few boarding pupils to feed each day, Fannie would walk to farm houses nearby and beg for food supplies to feed the children.

help support a Christian school for black young people.

At the closing of the spring school term in 1918, much to the surprise of everyone at the mass gathering on the last day, Bowser announced his resignation from the school. He had been invited to go to Louisville, Kentucky, to work with the Highland Church of Christ in establishing a work among blacks there. E. L. Jorgensen was the minister for that church and they had sponsored mission work in Africa with a Frenchman named Don Carlos Janes. Janes had visited with Bowser in

Nashville before the Silver Point school had been started and showed slides of his African work and aroused his interest.

Bowser decided to move from Silver Point leaving the frustrations of the school behind, and hoping for a better situation in Louisville. Some people in Nashville had complained that the school was too remote a location, and that it had no farms to support itself or to provide part-time jobs.

After Bowser left, Henry Clay and S. W. Womack took the lead in trying to rally more support for the school. Silver Point Christian Institute held on as a Christian school for two more years. The last report in the *Gospel Advocate* was from L. W. Lankford on January 15, 1920,[15] indicating that the school was barely making ends meet. That spring saw the last of the school as it was known to be connected with the churches of Christ. It had lasted for thirteen years which was an amazing feat for the times and circumstances. The brick building continued to house the church and served as a public school many years afterwards under the guidance of the teachers Bowser trained. But Bowser's departure marked the end of an era. He was sadly missed by both black and whites in the community. The focus of attention regarding Christian education then began to turn back to Nashville—the geographic center of the brotherhood.

Southern Practical Institute

While reluctant to see Silver Point school efforts die, Womack could not but commend a new effort

FURTHER EDUCATIONAL EFFORTS

by Burton to establish a Christian school for blacks in Nashville. He wrote in favor of the Southern Practical Institute which was planned to open January 5, 1920, when he wrote to the *Gospel Advocate* on January 1, 1920.[16] In the fall of 1919, Annie Tuggle, by then back in the Memphis area, received a letter from Burton announcing that he was purchasing a building which would be donated to educate black youngsters in literary and industrial trades. He asked her to canvass in the tri-states for students for the school.[7] With funds being provided by Burton, Tuggle worked toward the school's opening in January. A short time later, word came to her that Silver Point was to close and that Bowser was being urged by Burton to head the Bible teaching in the school in Nashville.

Bowser had since settled in Louisville and was being warmly received. He was quite reluctant to leave. He did, however, agree to go to Nashville for the opening of the new school and tentatively serve as its principal. He left his family in Louisville, but brought Nate Hogan (age sixteen) with him and enrolled him in the school. He planned to move the rest of the family to Nashville if circumstances in the school were favorable. Burton needed help around his house and so provided a room for Hogan. He later heard Hogan preach and was much impressed.

The school building itself was a large three-story frame building at 613 Ewing Avenue and contained forty rooms. It had the potential to be not only a literary institution, but also a location for teaching many trades as well. Burton was a generous benefactor and an important church leader who was dedicated to Christian education for both blacks and whites. He had provided a significant opportunity for blacks by establishing this new school.

In order to secure the goodwill and support of the whites, Burton appointed C. E. W. Dorris, his friend and a well-known preacher, as superintendent. Bowser was the principal, and was in charge of academics—especially the Bible classes. The first day saw about forty boarding students and many more day students enroll. Tuggle had done an effective job in recruiting most of the boarding students. But the bright prospects for the school turned sour before the first week was over.

Bowser was upset to see the black students being told to enter the school by the back door. This, of course, was a universal custom of the segregated South, and Dorris insisted that it should be carried out at the school too. When Bowser objected, Dorris replied that many whites from all over the city would be coming to visit the school and they would be offended if blacks were allowed to enter by the front door. Dorris reasoned that they entered white homes and most businesses by the back door, and so it should be at the school. Dorris insisted that the support of the whites demanded the practice, and he would be ashamed if his friends came and saw it otherwise. Bowser said it was a black school and he would not subject the pupils to such indignity in their own school. Keeble urged Bowser to let the pupils enter through the back door. He told Bowser they would still be getting the Christian education they so much desired. But Bowser could not accept it.[18]

FURTHER EDUCATIONAL EFFORTS

At the end of the week, he took young Hogan with him and went back to Louisville. Bowser felt so strongly about the issue that he urged the blacks not to further support the school under these conditions.

Bowser's influence was so great that others followed his lead to such an extent that the school was forced to close permanently at the end of six weeks. Before the year 1920 ended, blacks in the Nashville churches had rallied to make a downpayment on some property in north Nashville for a school.[19] But it was twenty years before the school became a reality in the Nashville Christian Institute.

[1]G. P. Bowser, "Work Among the Colored People," *Gospel Advocate* 54(29 February 1912):279.
[2]Ibid., 34(4 July 1912):793.
[3]Ibid., 55(1 May 1913):431.
[4]Ibid.
[5]Ibid., p. 45.
[6]Tuggle, *Another World Wonder*, p. 47.
[7]S. W. Womack, "Among the Colored People," *Gospel Advocate* 55(1 May 1913):431.
[8]G. P. Bowser, "The Colored Bible School," *Gospel Advocate* 56(7 May 1914):508.
[9]A. M. Burton, "The Prospects and Needs of the Putnam County Industrial School for Negroes," *Gospel Advocate* 58(10 February 1916):132.
[10]S. W. Womack, "Report for January and February," *Gospel Advocate* 58 (6 April 1916):354,355; G. P. Bowser, "The Colored School at Silver Point," *Gospel Advocate* 58(4 May 1916):458.
[11]"Report of Silver Point Bible School for Negroes," *Gospel Advocate* 58(27 July 1916):748.
[12]Tuggle, *Another World Wonder*, p. 48.
[13]S. P. Pittman, "Obligations to the Colored Race," *Gospel Advocate* 59 (9 August 1917):762.

[14]G. P. Bowser, "Communication from G. P. Bowser," *Gosvel Advocate* 59(6 September 1917):876.
[15]L. W. Lankford, "The School at Silver Point," *Gospel Advocate* 62(15 January 1920):67.
[16]S. W. Womack, "Among the Colored Folks," *Gospel Advocate* 62(1 January 1920):22.
[17]Tuggle, *Another World Wonder*, p. 62.
[18]Idem, Thelma Holt.
[19]Tuggle, *Another World Wonder*, p. 132.

CHAPTER 5

Bowser's Quest Continues

The Move to Louisville

When Don Carlos Janes came to Nashville before Bowser's Silver Point days and showed slides of his work, it seemed to have had a special fascination for Bowser. For one thing, Janes depicted modern Africans in civilized dress, not as savages. Most textbooks adhered to the latter concept. At one point while in the Methodist Church, Bowser had prepared to do mission work in Africa. For a long time, he had dreamed of his ancestoral homeland and hoped someday to go there. He had prayed for the success of Marcus Garvey who had advocated the dignity of the black man as coming from highly civilized African roots and urged the deportation of these former slaves back to their homeland. The interest in Africa by the Highland Church of Christ in Louisville showed new and challenging possibilities for Bowser.

The congregation wanted Bowser to move to Louisville to establish a church among blacks. E. L. Jorgensen, the minister, had been going into the homes of black people on Sunday afternoons and teaching them the gospel. A house was rented for

Bowser and his family—then comprised of Thelma and Nate Hogan, both sixteen; Lucille, eleven; and Philista, eight. Plans were then made for their work to begin there in the city, but the preliminary plans did not include a school.

The first Sunday in Louisville was quite an experience for this black family from the South. Having been accustomed to the rigid rules of segregation, they were unsure what treatment to expect from a community still on the southern side of the Ohio River. But before they came to worship with the Highland congregation, they asked if their presence would be permissible. "Why, yes. Come on in!" was the reply. The ushers were apparently expecting Bowser, because he was taken to the front of the auditorium to the pulpit to be seated. The rest of the family was also taken up to the front of the building. They were not told to take a back seat as they expected. It was very uplifting to be welcomed by white people and treated with such dignity. Certainly there was a different racial climate here than that which they had known before. This new attitude certainly felt good for them. E. L. Jorgensen along with Brother Janes seemed to take the lead in this spirit in the congregation, and they both obviously desired the Bowser family's happiness and friendship.

For the first few Sundays, the Bowsers worshiped with the Highland congregation in the mornings and then continued Jorgensen's habit of visiting in black homes in the afternoons with a service. As Bowser began to think about establishing the new church, he walked up and down the streets passing out tracts. He engaged in discussions and soon people gathered around. He also used his daughter Thelma who had a good singing voice. He had her begin singing until a crowd gathered and then he began telling them about the one true church of the Bible. Afterward, he invited the crowd to the place of worship which had been secured on Burnett Avenue. It was a lovely building in the black community, and it was not long before a growing group began to assemble each Lord's Day.

Fannie did domestic work for the Jorgensens. The family consisted of only "Brother Jorgensen" and "Mrs. Jorgensen", as they were called. The difference in racial attitudes was reflected in how they were addressed. He was warm and friendly, but Mrs. Jorgensen's manner demanded a more formal name. When Fannie prepared dinner, Brother Jorgensen insisted that the three eat together. He reasoned to Fannie, "We don't eat when we have guests in the house unless they eat too." Unhappy with that, Mrs. Jorgensen always made some excuse not to be present at the dinner table to eat with a black person.

Fannie was an excellent laundress. She got a job with one of the exclusive stores in town—W. K. Stewart Dry Goods. There she was bonded to guarantee quality workmanship. Very expensive items were brought to her by special delivery and she carefully hand washed them, ironed the delicate pleats, and made them ready to be put back on the shelf for sale.

Through some of her work in decorating, word

got around that she was talented in this area, and she was contacted by rich families to assist when a decorator was brought in. The time soon came when Fannie's approval was sought by many before a decision was made. She definitely possessed a natural talent along this line. Everywhere she lived she had to earn money, and she always found something to do. She always did her best and took pride in her work. As a result, her work was appreciated and respected.

Since the Burnett Avenue Church of Christ was a mission work out of the Highland congregation, the Bowser family had a great deal of contact with the home congregation. The business meetings at that time included both men and women, and all of the Bowsers attended. Later, Thelma was asked to take the minutes of these meetings. At a meeting one evening, Jorgensen became so filled with emotion as he thought about Bowser with all his talent and abilities and what he suffered for the Lord that he came over and hugged and kissed him.

In Louisville, Jorgensen and Janes were associated with a Christian journal called the *Word and Work*, and were associated with brethren who believed in premillennialism. This doctrine never interested Bowser very much and he knew it was controversial and too complicated to be of concern to most of the black brethren. He tended not to let it be an issue for division by coming out for or against it. He preferred to stress the plain teachings of the Scriptures where no argument existed. He felt that belief in premillennialism did not effect one's eternal salvation.

BOWSER'S QUEST CONTINUES

In 1920, Bowser was persuaded to come from Louisville to investigate becoming the main Bible teacher for the Southern Christian Institute in Nashville. A. M. Burton was purchasing a large, old school building for the purpose of educating black youngsters and had installed a white preacher as the Principal. The Principal refused to let the pupils enter the school by the front door which irritated Bowser. Bowser left after a week, taking young Nate Hogan, his 'adopted' son who was 14, with him.

Because these brethren were in the printing business with the journal and Sunday school literature, Bowser let them assist him in the printing of the

Echo. This was the first help that any whites had given to the paper and it endeared their friendship to him. It was also in the *Christian Echo* in 1927 that Bowser estimated that there were twenty-six black congregations of the churches of Christ with a total membership of 1,165.[1]

Because Louisville presented such a different experience for Bowser—a time of peace wherein he could reflect on his labors thus far—he wrote in the *Gospel Advocate* from Louisville in 1924:

> It has often occurred to me that if the white brethren of the church of Christ would suggest to us definite plans and cooperate with us in fostering, building and maintaining schools, as whites among the denominations are doing for the colored, it would indeed be 'bread cast upon waters' that would be seen for many days hence.[2]

It is clear that his dream of establishing a Christian school for his people had not died. But there is no indication that he made any attempts to teach anyone outside of his family and usual church responsibilities during the few years he was in Louisville. It was several years before he again attempted to establish a school. True to his earlier statement, when he did make the next attempt in Fort Smith, Arkansas, he did not seriously attempt to look to whites for support.

Bowser Family Matters

Fannie had two brothers who died when they were quite young men. One had come to Louisville with his second wife. The Bowsers were able to house him in a rear apartment in a building used to print the *Echo* which was located on the back of the place where they lived. The brother died while living there.

It was also in Louisville that Lucille, the Bowser's sixteen-year-old daughter, died during an epileptic seizure. Wherever they had been, Fannie had constantly searched for a doctor who might be able to help Lucille. Very little was known about epilepsy at the time, but various remedies were tried without success. Hot mustard plasters were used on her wrists and ankles, but only resulted in scar tissue. When she had attacks at school, her friends gathered around and held her hands and feet until the seizure passed. But despite her mother's efforts, Lucille passed away.

During the summer of 1918, Thelma (sixteen) and her father went to Detroit for their second visit. The first visit had been when she was thirteen. Nate Hogan had gone home to Arkansas as he usually did when school was out, so Bowser traveled with Thelma. After World War I, thousands of people, both black and white, flocked to the North—especially to Detroit where good wages were offered. The money that could be made there far surpassed that which could be earned on the farms. Bowser pitched a tent there and aided the young church in reaching the community for Christ. Thelma did more singing on the sidewalks as her father passed out tracts. When a crowd gathered, Bowser preached a few words and then invited the people to the meeting.

UNDYING DEDICATION

Attendance was fairly good each evening, and one young man attending every night took a special interest in the preacher's daughter. He invited Thelma to a few movies at first, and then asked her to go to Belle Isle—the city park in the Detroit River. Because one reached the showplace only by boat in those days, Thelma, who had never been in the water and couldn't swim, agreed to go only if accompanied by her father since he could swim. Bowser consented to go with them at the appointed time.

In the meantime, the young man told Thelma he had a friend he wanted her to meet. She told her father where she was going and, they left to go and meet the friend. Upon arriving at the lady's house, the woman said, "This is a fine looking girl. Is she from Detroit?" He lied and said she was and the lady replied that his room was ready. Thelma was apprehensive, but she allowed him to lead her to a bedroom. He said he wanted to talk to her, but it was soon obvious that he had other things in mind.

Thelma sat him down, pointed her finger at him, and lectured him soundly on his ungodly intentions. He apologized and said he would not do it again. Although she liked him, she never dated him again. Bowser and Fannie had a good relationship with their children and had discussed sex with Thelma in addition to providing her with good literature to read. She later reflected that if she had done anything wrong, it would have been with her eyes wide open.

During the last years at Silver Point, a bright young preaching student courted Thelma. His name was Marion Francis Holt and he was the son of the Holts from Marshall County, Tennessee who had been impressed with Bowser's preaching many years ago. Marion was a good speaker and showed great promise in the work for the church. The Bowsers were pleased with the match, for it illustrated what they believed—young people should marry in the church. Their oldest daughter, Clara, had not done so and it had been a disappointment. Marion had planned to finish two years of college at Jarvis Christian College in Hawkins, Texas, which was operated by the Christian Church for blacks, but instead he promised to take a job in Indianapolis so he could get married.

E. L. Jorgensen was selected to perform the wedding and there were more whites than blacks at the ceremony. The wedding was held on Sunday afternoon and the couple left immediately for Indianapolis, where his job started the next morning. The young Holts did not stay there long, but went back to his home in Tennessee where he farmed and taught school while they began their family. Later Marion was asked to become the minister for the Jackson Street Church of Christ in Nashville where he had a long and fruitful ministry. But after six children had been born and twenty-three years together, the marriage ended in divorce.

Two Disciples

After getting the church started in Louisville, Bowser looked for new horizons. He never wanted to settle permanently in any one place since he considered himself to be an evangelist. Although the *Echo* for November, 1931[3] seems to have come from Louisville, Bowser spent some time in early spring of the same year in Fort Worth. It was while he was in Fort Worth that he became acquainted with a young blind Baptist preacher whom Bowser discovered to have a deep and sincere interest in the word of God. The man's name was George Edmond Steward and he became one of the most respected Bible scholars of the black church.

The young preacher was holding a revival in Bowser's neighborhood when they first met. The two were immediately attracted to one another and engaged in many discussions of the Scriptures. "Blind Steward," as he became known, began attending the Bible classes which Bowser conducted and was impressed as the Bible truths were skillfully punctuated with many quotations from the text. In March of 1931, Bowser held a gospel meeting with the church in which Steward was baptized.[4] After his leaving the Baptists, Bowser helped Steward obtain a few preaching appointments with churches. Under Bowser's guidance, the young man learned faster than any new convert he had ever taught.

In 1930, Marshall Keeble was on the payroll of A. M. Burton to evangelize for the Lord wherever he could. He came to Fort Smith, Arkansas, and conducted a very successful gospel meeting in which eighty-six persons were baptized. This prompted J. W. Brents, the white preacher for the Spaulding Boulevard Church of Christ in Muskogee, Oklahoma, to invite Keeble to his town for a two-week meeting. It resulted in two hundred and four baptisms—the most successful evangelistic series in Keeble's career and in the history of the church of Christ among blacks.

One woman and her son were quite happy because up until that time, although raised in the church of Christ in Arkansas, she had been only able to worship with the instrumental Christian church since there was no church of Christ there. Her name had been Julia Winston before her remarriage after her first husband died, and her teenaged son was John Steve Winston.[5] Young Winston became one of Bowser's most devoted and active "Timothys" and led efforts to carry on Bowser's educational thrust.

Winston had been raised mainly by his devout uncle who was an elder in the church of Christ in Arkansas. The young man's interest and enthusiasm for the church—especially as a song leader—was greatly appreciated when Bowser came to visit the mushrooming new church. Bowser was also then helpful in securing Nate Hogan, who had left the church for a while but who had returned with renewed spiritual determination, to come and take the leadersip in preaching and developing this new congregation. This further encouraged Winston in his growth in the faith. Hogan and Winston, as preacher and song leader, together planted the congregation in Okmulgee in 1934 with a two-week meeting which produced one hundred eighty-nine baptisms.

UNDYING DEDICATION

[1] G. P. Bowser, *Christian Echo* (20 January 1927) as quoted in Stephen D. Eckstein, Jr., *The History of the Churches of Christ in Texas* (Austin: Firm Foundation Publishing House), 1963.

[2] G. P. Bowser, "The Outlook Among the Colored People," *Gospel Advocate* 66(30 October 1924):1064.

[3] Ibid., Eckstein, p. 314.

[4] Interview with G. E. Steward, Pontiac, Michigan, 1975.

[5] Interview with J. S. Winston, Detroit, Michigan, 30 March 1973.

CHAPTER 6

A New Endeavor

Fort Smith and Levi Kennedy

By 1933, Bowser, Fannie, and Philista (age twenty-three) had moved to Fort Smith, Arkansas to work with the church there. Bowser enlisted the aid of three leading preachers—R. N. Hogan, G. E. Steward, and Paul English—to help him build a Christian school in Fort Smith.[1] The Nashville brethren, even though unable financially to establish a school as yet, decided not to sell the property they had bought earlier for a school and give its resources to Bowser. Since Bowser's friends could not presuade the Nashville brethren to help the new school in 1933 and 1934, there was very little support—especially from Christians east of the Mississippi during the Depression. But Bowser still did not let his dream die.

In 1933, Levi Kennedy—a young man raised in the church in Hickman County, Tennessee, and the son of a gospel preacher—was traveling from his home in Chicago and stopped to visit Bowser in Fort Smith. Kennedy had been devout and faithful in the church all of his thirty-five years, drove a pie truck for a living, and he had heard Bowser preach back home in Hickman County. Kennedy had begun to give a few talks in the church himself. So Bowser asked him to speak. As they walked home afterwards, Bowser said, "Well, well, well. I didn't know you could do that well. If you go back to Chicago and get on that truck and don't get out and help us do this missionary work, you're going to die and go to hell!"

Kennedy knew Bowser's reputation and had great respect for his opinion. He did not have to ponder long on what Bowser had said—it was a fact! He went back to Chicago a changed man.[2] After a brief and unpleasant experience with the church in Muskogee, Oklahoma, Kennedy went back to serve the Lord effectively in and out of Chicago until he died in 1971.

Eventually, Bowser decided to open a school himself by taking in whatever students he could gather and supporting the school as best he could. In this endeavor he showed great spiritual fortitude. Bowser was sixty-four years of age and Fannie was sixty-nine in 1938 when he opened classes that fall. He had twenty-three neighboring children ranging in ages from five to thirteen.[3] He appealed through the *Christian Echo:*

It is grievous as well as shameful to think of 30,000 Negro disciples and not a school among us. When will our people throw off the "yoke of indifference" and decide to do something to educate our boys and girls under Christian influence? Our white brethren from the beginning of the Restoration, saw the need for schools and at once went to work with telling results. Will you preachers please line up

A NEW ENDEAVOR

with me in a determined way for a Christian school? Let me hear from you.[4]

Later he was given the use of the Ninth Street Church of Christ in which to conduct his classes. Upon hearing of the school, young preachers began to come from different places for training. Most of them were already married and came with their families. They wanted to study from the best teacher available to them—and this was Bowser. Blacks still were not allowed into white Christian schools except the newly-opened, and somewhat remote Pepperdine College In Los Angeles, California. If these young men and their families did not have money (and most didn't), they stayed with the Bowsers in their home and ate at their table. Some stayed in homes of church members in town.

There was a little money available to students if they worked in the print shop that Bowser operated. It was there that the *Echo* was printed. At first, the printing was done with hand-set, 10-point single type. Then Bowser used a Lawton type and finally had the *Echo* linotyped so he could run it off on his large-roller press.[5] Anyone who was available pitched in and got the job done in work-party fashion. Every student who attended school was expected to help set type and run the press. Bowser believed that a preacher ought to do something else besides preach, so he also taught printing. But as far as it is known, only two of his pupils ever became professional printers.

In 1939, Bowser's daughter, Thelma Holt, sent

The three Bowser children. Standing left to right: Clara Scaggs, Philista Folke and seated, Thelma Holt. The picture was taken in Fort Smith, Arkansas when the girls came to visit their parents.

her son George Phillip Holt (also known as "G. P.") to live with his grandparents. He was sixteen at the time. As a single parent, she was struggling to make a living and care for her children. She felt it would be good for the boy to be under his grandfather's influence. So he was enrolled in the school. He studied the Bible and learned to set type along with the rest of the students. Inspired by that environment and especially influenced by a fellow student, O. B. Butler—an accomplished speaker—Holt preached his first sermon before the year elapsed. Bowser's grandson was also a natural choice to accompany Bowser in his travels from June to September.

Bowser gave his grandson twenty-five cents a day but fussed about it, saying he didn't need it. Holt earned a little extra money through selling some of the tracts, song books, or other printed matter which Bowser had produced. The small booklet, "What We Believe and Why We Believe It," went through several editions and was widely circulated with the help of Holt and others.

More Travels

In the early 1930s, Bowser conducted a gospel meeting in the Birmingham, Alabama suburb of Titusville. He stayed with the Nall family, members of the local church.[6] On Sunday afternoon when lunch was over, Bowser took a chair out to the sidewalk in this residential neighborhood. As people passed, he pointed to the Bible lying open in the chair, and began to preach. Some of the church members were a little embarrassed, but Bowser was undaunted. He was doing God's work and this was his way of advertising the meeting. Gradually, a few stopped to listen.

He baited the denominationalists with questions about their beliefs and what their preachers were teaching. Quoting the Bible extensively, he exposed error in human traditions. He urged them to come to the afternoon meeting in the church building at 3:00 P.M. After this service, with the open Bible and the chair, he continued on the street until time for the evening service.

His badgering of sectarians resulted in a debate in this location which was attended by both white and black Christians in the Birmingham area. Bowser was very dogmatic in his denunciation of all religious practice not consistent with New Testament Christianity. His name-calling of sectarians sometimes made it difficult for the church members who had to live with their neighbors after Bowser left town. But his method did provoke some religious-minded people to search the Scriptures—either to find the truth for themselves or to try and justify their beliefs and practices.

On one occasion, J. S. Winston was driving Bowser through west Tennessee when they passed through Brownsville on a Saturday afternoon. This was the county seat town for Haywood County, which contained one of the largest black populations in the state. The court square was packed with people. It was a Saturday custom there that after a hard week on the farm, people came to town to shop and socialize for most of the day. Seeing

A NEW ENDEAVOR

Bowser drove a rattle-trap Model-T Ford around the country preaching, including a trip to California. When he passed through Texas, it broke down and he called on Reuel Lemmons in Cleburne to help him with repairs.

the crowds, Bowser was overwhelmed. He said to Winston, "Pull her (the car) over and stop her. Look at all these people. They must hear the gospel!"

He got out and fumbled in the back for an old rag with some writing on it. Charging Winston to hold up the chart, he called out, "Hear me!" and began preaching. This continued until it got too dark to see the words of the chart.[7] Bowser and Winston stayed there long enough to baptize a few people. After locating a preacher for them, they moved on.

Sometime in the 1930s, Bowser was invited by

mistake to the New Zion Christian Church in east Texas. After three days, the white brethren sent to Missouri for a man to come and debate Bowser. The man's name was Abe Young, but he was no match for Bowser's experienced defense of his views. Bowser persuaded the Christian church to invite R. N. Hogan from Fort Worth, and later, J. S. Winston to come and preach for them. Bowser found about twenty congregations—all of the "digressive" persuasion. Together, these three men joined forces to bring them to the church of Christ.

The Christian Church brethren in Texas saw nothing wrong with accepting people of denominational backgrounds into their fellowship. They called it "shaking" them into the church with a handshake, regardless of the nature or mode of baptism. Many of these churches not only used the instrument, but had been established with one man as an elder who controlled his church. These beliefs were in the area of Jarvis Christian College influence. Bowser, Hogan, and Winston were quite successful in "capturing" these churches away from the Christian church's influence.

Ray Jennings[8] tells of the time around 1936 when as a young man in Lebanon, Tennessee working at the Castle Heights Military Academy, he first met Bowser. After getting off from work in the afternoons he rode his bicycle toward the town square on his way home. There by the court house, he saw a cluster of people and he went over to investigate. The center of the interest was Bowser's preaching. Every day while Bowser was in town for the gospel meeting, he held this sort of public discussion. Quite a group would gather to listen.

A NEW ENDEAVOR

The crowd was polite and there was no badgering or name-calling. Those who took the time to hear his message sensed his seriousness and skill in his many quotes from the Bible. After about an hour he urged the people to come and hear him preach in the building of the church of Christ that evening. Jennings went, although his father was a long-time preacher for the Holiness church in town. Jennings was eventually won to the church of Christ.

Reuel Lemmons, editor of the *Firm Foundation*, remembers a time when he was preaching in Cleburne, Texas, and Bowser came through on his way out west. His old car broke down and he needed some help to get on his way. The congregation helped to get Bowser on the bus. The car, which been completely worn out, was sold and the money was sent to Bowser.[9]

Another trip found Bowser traveling in his model-T when a tire came off and caused the car to swerve and be jostled severely until it came to a stop. Bowser and Fannie immediately began gathering the copies of the *Echo* and the tracts that had been scattered by the wind. They had little regard for their plight, so great was their concern that the papers not be lost.

Later when Bowser was being driven by his grandson, G. P. Holt,[10] they came to Little Rock, Arkansas. E. R. Harper was the preacher for the Sixth and Izard Church of Christ there. Harper helped Bowser put up a tent for a revival in the black community, but when Bowser and Holt came to Harper's gospel meeting for the daytime services, Harper met them on the front steps and said it would be wise for them not to come in. It was clear that there was still a great amount of prejudice there. But Bowser continued his travels and preaching in the area.

[1] Ibid., Evans, p. 6.
[2] Interview with Levi Kennedy, Chicago, Illinois around 1969.
[3] J. S. Winston's *Memoirs* as quoted in Evans, p. 7.
[4] G. P. Bowser in *Christain Echo*, 1938 as quoted in *Life and Times of G. P. Bowser* by Thelma Holt, p. 27.
[5] Interview with G. P. Holt, Sr., Detroit, Michigan, 24 May 1973.
[6] Interview with Juliett Manuel, Detroit, Michigan, 22 November 1977.
[7] Idem, Winston.
[8] Interview with Ray Jennings, Detroit, Michigan 20 April 1983.
[9] Idem, Lemmons.
[10] Idem, G. P. Holt.

CHAPTER 7

The Fruits of Labor

Bowser Christian Institute

Seeing the great determination of Bowser to start a school, J. S. Winston, as the minister for the church of Christ in Sherman, Texas, called a meeting of church leaders in Dallas to organize the financial drive to back the school. The meeting was held November 9, 1938, in the church building of the Oak Cliff Church of Christ. It was attended mostly by preachers of the Dallas area. A collection of one hundred fifty dollars was taken and sent immediately to Bowser who put fifty dollars of it as downpayment on a three-story frame building which he used as a school building. It was a large structure of about fifteen rooms, with a smaller building behind it. Both buildings provided six classrooms and a boys dormitory, which housed thirty-one boys in 1939.[1]

Bowser was greatly encouraged by Winston's efforts and he suggested that Winston try next for a national meeting of church leaders to support the school. This meeting was held in November of 1939 in Fort Smith. It was attended by fifteen preachers from different parts of the United States. A board of directors was established for the guidance of the school—G. E. Steward, R. N. Hogan, Levi Kennedy, and T. H. Busby.[2] "Bowser Christian Institute" was adopted as the formal name and about two hundred dollars was raised for the school during the meeting.

As the student body increased, two female teachers were added to the faculty. One was Mrs. Maud Penny who taught English and math. The other is not known. At the school a typical day started with breakfast. Since everything was done in that one building, everyone ate in the dining hall. Classes began around 8:00 and lasted until 3:30. They had only one break—lunch. There were a few female students and they lived with the Bowsers, who had a separate house nearby.

There was a great emphasis given to preaching and defending the truth of the Bible. Since there were many attacks on the church, Bowser wanted to prepare the young people for when they went out into the field. He emphasized memorization of the Bible as he himself had done. The preachers were required to memorize a chapter from the Old Testament one week and a chapter from the New Testament the next.

In practicing Bible study with the students, Bowser had them quote a passage from somewhere in the Bible and then he gave the verse before and after it. Bowser was so good at this that the students often tried to catch him in a mistake but never could. Occasionally, a student tried to mix some passages together or paraphrase a text, but Bowser always caught it and quoted the Bible correctly.[3]

THE FRUITS OF LABOR

Some of the students had part-time jobs after school. If not working, the students studied or played ball for the rest of the day or evening. Fort Smith was not a large town, so there was not much to do off campus.

The school year of 1939–1940 was the high point of the Bowser Christian Institute. Tuition was free, and room and board cost fourteen dollars per month with one hundred fifty dollars needed for incidental expenses. The curriculum embraced grades from kindergarten through high school, and included a special instruction program for ministers and church workers. The Bible, of course, was a fundamental text used every day along with secular subjects.[4]

World War II saw the nation's attention and resources focused on war. Bowser suffered severely from poverty during this time, but he determined to keep the school alive. This he did by trusting the Lord to supply his needs. Many days there would not be any food left at the end of the day. Bowser went about his business as usual, and didn't open the day's mail until after supper was finished. Some days there was as little as fifty cents or one dollar in the mail, but it enabled them to buy some food for the next day. Then they waited for the next day's mail to be opened.

Bowser also went to merchants in town and asked for donations which they gladly gave. Each year there was a flood and merchants paid students from the school to help move their merchandise. They also donated foodstuffs to the school in appreciation for this help.

Lectureship time was the highlight of the year,

not only because of the many visitors and great preaching, but also because men like Winston came in cars loaded with food and other donations to the school.

Sometimes churches or individuals ordered tracts or hymnals from which a little profit was gained. In 1942, Bowser printed a national *Directory of the Churches of Christ, Colored* which he sold for fifteen cents each. He listed 337 congregations and 352 preachers. When the information was available, he listed the address, number of members, approximate value of the church buildings, and the number of members added to the church in 1942.[5] This venture also brought the school a profit.

In the fall of 1942, Winston invited Annie Tuggle to come and help with the school. She came and stayed for several weeks, and did some traveling in Oklahoma in behalf of funds.[6] Bowser did a lot of preaching, going almost every weekend to a congregation with some of his preaching students. Often these young men preached for about ten minutes before Bowser got up to speak. Travel to these places was usually done by car or sometimes by bus. Often it took the entire weekend to accomplish such a trip.

In 1944, Thelma Holt left Detroit for a two-week trip to visit her parents in Fort Smith. She ended up staying two years. When she saw her aging parents and what they were still trying to do on such a small and undependable income, she determined not to leave there until she had brought relief to them. Thelma wrote her oldest daughter to send her things and to bring the rest of the family to Fort

THE FRUITS OF LABOR

The front page of the Christian Echo, May 20, 1945 which contains the photograph of the First National Lectureship in 1945. These lectureships have been a factor in unifying and strengthening the brotherhood among blacks.

Smith. Every church leader Thelma contacted knew she meant business. Bowser was seventy years old and Fannie was seventy-five. The school operated for two more years while Thelma wrestled with the problem of how to relieve her parents.

She found life in Fort Smith to be hard as she

tried to help the school while she was there. She took over the job of matron to the girls. Sometimes at night some of the boys slipped out to the red-light district in town. Thelma roused Maud Penny out of bed and the two of them drove to the location of the black policeman on duty and asked him to help them locate the truants and bring them back to school.

Finally Thelma took the bull by the horns and sold the property, thus ending the school in 1946. Winston said to her "Babe, you're putting us out of business!" Thelma said "Yes, because you are not in business."

She explained in detail the plight of her parents, saying that they were not going to complain. They realized then that she had to close the school.[7] With the sale of the property, the school debts were liquidated and the balance of the money was given to move the Bowsers to go Detroit and live with their daughter, Philista.

During the move, there was an unfortunate loss to history. The local moving company in Fort Smith was contracted to take the Bowser possessions to Detroit. En route, there was an accident and some of Bowser's boxes were lost. They contained books, papers, and records which he hoped to use in writing a book of the history of the church. He had also carried a camera with him and had taken many pictures. These were also lost. The lost copies of the *Echo* were, of course, irreplacable. The moving company was asked if there was anything saved, but they never produced anything.

THE FRUITS OF LABOR

Life in Detroit

Bowser rode to Detroit in his car, but Fannie traveled by train for a more comfortable trip. She suffered from a heart problem and was crippled with arthritis. She could walk only very slowly. The Bowsers had lived in Detroit only a short while when the local brethren urged him to begin teaching. Plans were made to open the Bowser Christian Institute in the educational wing of the Joseph Campau Church of Christ. This congregation had taken over a large old Lutheran church building which had a separate building beside it for use as a school. Local church leaders were glad to have Bowser in their midst as a teacher and so encouraged the effort.

Between the time of their moving to Detroit in 1946 and the opening of the school in the fall of 1947, a great deal of money and effort was spent in converting part of the educational building into a dormitory. Donations were received for furnishing the rooms. After the school opened, Bowser taught Bible and was assisted by his daughter Thelma. Plans called for setting up a grammar school and a high school with teachers certified by the state of Michigan. Bowser could not rest when there was an opportunity to teach the Bible to young people. He wrote in the *Echo* as he urged support for the new school:

> Christianity is the only remedy that will completely solve the many problems of our age, therefore Christian education is a dire necessity of this age.

UNDYING DEDICATION

In 1950, shortly before his death of cancer, the ailing Bowser was driven by J. S. Winston in the back seat of Winston's car, propped with pillows, out to Terrell, Texas to see the property which the brethren had secured for the beginning of the new school, Southwestern Christian College.

We hear a great deal about juvenile delinquency these days, and those who are greatly concerned about it are seeking a remedy for it, but we have had a remedy for many years. Christianity is not a new modern religion, but a rich heritage which has come down to us from ancient days. We need only to apply the remedy for educating our young people in the principles of primitive Christianity, so that they may grow up to be better citizens, good Christians, and profitable servants of suffering humanity. Only in this way will we ever completely eliminate that great evil known as juvenile delinquency.

Bowser Christian Institute is preparing to play its part

well in the great work of educating people in the divine principles of primitive Christianity. Our doors are open to all worthy boys and girls.[8]

The school began with some boarding students, and some others from local churches. When approval was sought from the Board of Education for accreditation, it was denied.[9] E. W. Anderson, who had his college degree, was appointed as principal. But the school board had a strong desire to upgrade educational standards and was adamantly against accreditation at a hearing set in downtown Detroit.

They insisted that Bowser attend Wayne State University before taking the certification test. Of course, he was not willing to do this at his age. Therefore the school closed, much to the hurt and disappointment of Bowser. He felt that the board at the institute had not backed him sufficiently. The school had lasted less than two years. But in that time, Bowser had managed to teach a few aspiring Bible students who valued his instruction.

Fort Worth

In June of 1947, Fannie died of a heart attack. Levi Kennedy came to give the eulogy. Bowser continued to preach and produce the *Echo* with Thelma's assistance. Realizing he was not going to continue the *Echo* much longer, he asked G. E. Steward to serve as editor. Eugene Smith, a white publisher of church materials in Dallas helped in the printing until he was killed in a plane crash.

Since Thelma's son Marion was a professional printer, it was hoped he would be able to serve as editor, but he didn't sufficiently work out as printer. So J. S. Winston helped put out a few issues. In June of 1949, Bowser asked Steward to send the responsibility for the *Echo* to R. N. Hogan in Los Angeles. It has been published there ever since.

It was through Bowser's work with the *Echo* that he knew of a woman who had been a good promoter in sending in subscriptions. He was quite lonely so he wrote asking the church where she attended to give him a report on her and see if she was interested in marriage. Thus he married Hettie Nero, knowing little about her and never having seen her. She thought he owned a house in Fort Smith and had hoped to go there and live. This began his second marriage.

Although not in the forefront of the effort, Bowser was delighted to see some of his closest younger associates have meetings in behalf of establishing a Christian school in Texas. With the help of white members, an interracial board was formed and it was agreed to begin a school at the Lake Como Church of Christ in Fort Worth, Texas. An army barrack was moved there and construction was done to convert it to a men's dormitory and class room space. J. S. Winston was named as president, G. C. Washington as dean, and Bowser was asked to head the Bible department.[10] This church was the first congregation to give Bowser a regular salary.

The school, Southern Bible Institute, was opened

on October 5, 1948, and since the classes were conducted at night, there were forty-one students enrolled. Considerable advertising gained monthly pledges and substantial funds accumulated for the college. By February of 1949, eleven thousand dollars had been spent toward getting the school in operation.[11]

Unfortunately, Bowser was injured in a car accident and also became sick with cancer. The doctors operated immediately to remove the cancer. His three daughters came to see about him and Thelma stayed to help look after their father. Church members sent donations to help pay for the medical bills. Hettie was afraid she might get cancer and so had difficulty in looking after Bowser once he came from the hospital. After about a year, the girls decided to take their father back to Detroit since his condition was becoming increasingly serious.

By the spring of 1950, the Southern Bible Institute leadership had purchased the land and property of the Texas Military School in Terrell, Texas. Plans were being made to open the school in the fall of 1950, with E. W. McMillan as president. J. S. Winston took the ailing Bowser out to Terrell to see the property and buildings where the present Southwestern Christian College now stands. Bowser was not even able to get out of the car, but he was pleased. His knew then that his dream would live on.

He went back to Detroit and lived with his daughters. On Sundays he was put in a chair and taken to Ford Avenue where he tried to preach short sermons while seated. He still wanted to teach the Word. He died on March 23, 1950. Levi Kennedy was again called by the family to preach the eulogy.

Thus ended the life of the most dedicated and influential man in Christian education among blacks. His life had certainly been an inspiration to all.

[1]*Christian Echo* (5 June 1944) p. 7; (5 September 1944) p. 7; Idem, G. P. Holt, Sr.
[2]Ibid., Evans, p. 8.
[3]Interview with Robert James, 23 April 1983.
[4]Ibid., Evans, p. 9.
[5]*Directory of the Churches of Christ, Colored* by G. P. Bowser, (Fort Smith, Arkansas: privately published, 1942).
[6]Ibid, *Another World Wonder*, p. 124.
[7]Idem, Thelma Holt interview.
[8]G. P. Bowser, *Christian Echo* (20 September 1947):1
[9]Interview with Mrs. D. J. Bynum, Detroit, Michigan, 29 October 1973.
[10]*Christian Echo* (5 October 1948):48.
[11]Ibid, (20 February 1949):8.

CONCLUSION

G. P. Bowser was a great man. He was compassionate, trustworthy, fervently evangelistic, faithful to the Bible, and firm in his resolve to help his people. He was also fairly easy to get along with, easily approached, humorous, and very likable. He hated the fact that his life was hindered by discrimination because of his race, but he was determined to put all things into God's hands. He was content with what the Lord provided and sought to do the best with what he had.

His greatest legacy comes from his undying dedication to the cause of Christian education. He recognized that he had been richly blessed in his native ability and training. He knew others could provide for the education of young people in a Christian setting and he longed for that opportunity to be a reality for his race. The work of Christ deserved the best training one could receive. Bowser never stopped working and planning for this goal.

A good case could be made for the fact that he lived ahead of his time. He was born when blacks had no money with which to support the good cause for which he gave himself. Perhaps he was not a good fund-raiser. Today this seems to be the chief skill needed in a Christian college president. It has always taken an unusual amount of energy to get a Christian school established. But the work of Bowser resulted in the existence of Southwestern Christian College in Terrell, Texas. Some of his pupils grew into preachers who shared some of his zeal to provide for a Christian school for future generations.

One cannot help but reflect on the divergent paths which the two great black leaders of the church of Christ took. They represented the ambivalence often felt by blacks when trying to function in a prejudiced white environment. Keeble sought to work with whites and Bowser, after he could not accept open discrimination, was content to work entirely among poor blacks.

The turning point with Bowser came as he returned to Nashville in 1920. A. M. Burton was trying to open the Southern Practical Institute and sought Bowser as the school's principal. Bowser could have worked under a white superintendent but he could not stand for black pupils to be forced to enter the school from the back door. That southern custom may have been tolerated in society, but Bowser did not want it to be the rule in the Christian school established for blacks. No amount of persuasion from his friends could change his mind.

Bowser knew that the school represented the best opportunity for a black school to be supported by whites of the churches of Christ. It would not have his blessing because it was demeaning to the

CONCLUSION

young boys and girl. He stood for something higher. From then on, Bowser never expected support from the white church for his school work. He continued to preach and dream of a better time.

After a ten-year waiting period, Bowser again attempted a Christian school in Fort Smith, Arkansas. This was his last sustained teaching period. Some of his former students were by this time able to bring in support primarily from black Christians. This cooperation among church leaders west of the Mississippi River led to the eventual establishment of Southwestern Christian College.

With the rise and fall of Nashville Christian Institute east of the Mississippi River, some of the momentum for Christian education among blacks was eventually transferred to Southwestern. Today, Southwestern Christian College enjoys national support from churches of Christ among blacks. It also receives support from interested whites. The school is a four-year accredited liberal arts school. Bowser's dream has become a living reality.

R. Vernon Boyd

www.ingramcontent.com/pod-product-compliance
Lightning Source LLC
LaVergne TN
LVHW011212080426
835508LV00007B/741